THE ASHBOUR BUXTON RAIL

By
C. T. GOODE

1990
ISBN 1 870313 08 9
72 Woodland Drive, Anlaby, Hull. HU10 7HX.

Contents

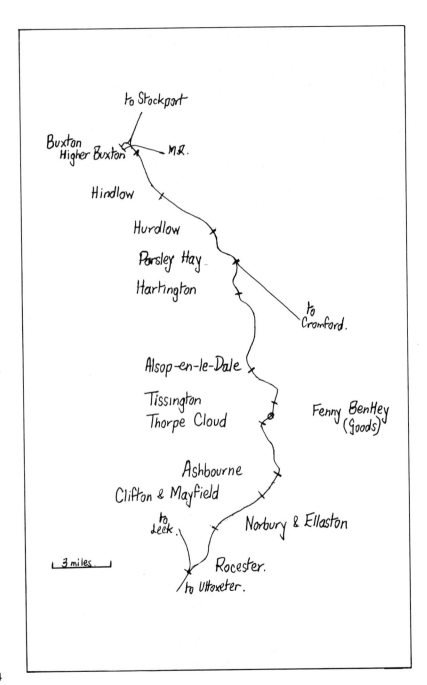

to Stockport

Buxton
Higher Buxton   M.R.

Hindlow

Hurdlow

Parsley Hay

Hartington
                                                    to
                                                    Cromford.

Alsop-en-le-Dale

Tissington
Thorpe Cloud   Fenny Bentley
                                    (goods)

Ashbourne

Clifton & Mayfield

            to
         Leek.   Norbury & Ellaston

3 miles

                    Rocester.
           to Uttoxeter.

FOREWORD

Although it has had something of an airing in recent writings, usually incidentally by authors who have tended to go overboard in their enthusiasm for the nearby Midland route with its air of solidity and its scenic charm, the LNWR branch between Ashbourne and Buxton has generally escaped the more thorough attention which I trust I have been able to give it, to reveal a line which proved itself to be of great value locally during its lifetime; a little eccentric perhaps, but in the very best Euston tradition.

My acknowledgements for kind assistance go to the National Railway Museum York, Derbyshire Records Office and the Derby and Buxton library staff. Messrs. Radford, Milward, Hewitt, Shemilt, Courtman and Wilson deserve mention for their help and interest.

As always happens once a book has been produced, more evidence appears and I should be grateful to hear from anyone with such material-or criticism-to offer.

C. Tony Goode.
Anlaby, Hull. 1990

Designed & Printed by
Swannack Brown & Co. Ltd.,
13a Anlaby Road, Hull.

—

The Ashbourne to Buxton Railway

Buxton is one of those hill-top settlements where one arrives wondering why it was ever sited in such a location, cold and wind-swept and featuring all too often in winter weather statistics as the coldest place in the country on a particular day. Of course, the blame can be laid at the door of the Romans who were adept at settling in such places, in this particular instance making a halt on the road to Manchester and lingering over the hot, medical springs to be found there, enjoying a pleasant, bracing climate during the summer. With the disappearance of the Romans the township declined, though the fame of the waters persisted, attracting, however, only small numbers of travellers. Among the famous was Mary, Queen of Scots, who managed to visit Buxton while in one of her many prisons, this time at Chatsworth. The town remained small, with less than two hundred dwellings in 1820, situated on the southern edge of the Pennines on its high gritstone moorland and limestone slopes. Its growth was slow, due to public awareness and, eventually, to the notice taken of it by the railway companies.

Interior of Buxton station, showing bookstall and, to the rear, one of the distinctive windows.   *Douglas Thompson*

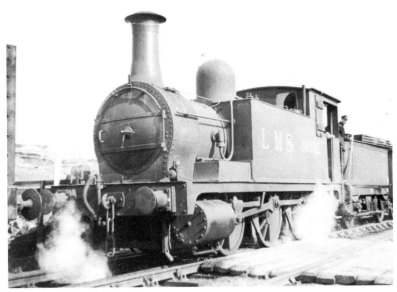

Ex North London Railway tank No. 58862 at Middleton on the C&HP line.
C.T. Goode

First of these was really more a part of the canal system than a railway, the Cromford & High Peak Company which crossed the Pennines very early in railway history, running from the Cromford canal in the valley of the Derwent for 33 miles up to a summit at Ladmanlow, then down to the Peak Forest canal in the Goyt valley west of Buxton. The original plan was to build a third canal to link the other two, but prohibitive costs likely to be involved in large scale engineering works, and a fear that water would be lost regularly through porous rock led to what might be seen now as a curious rail compromise of flat sections of route linked up by inclines - a canal bed with railway lines and beam engines instead of locks. The first survey, by Richard Wilson, was in 1814 and was virtually repeated in the one made by Josias Jessop later on. The shareholders approved and the necessary Act was passed in April 1825. A section of 15½ miles, from Cromford to Hurdlow, was opened for use in May 1830, with the last section to Whaley opened on 6th. July 1831. The line in fact took six years to build and was, as stated, 33 miles in length, with nine inclined planes. Machinery for these was supplied by the Butterley Iron Company of Ripley, later famous for the splendid ironwork in St. Pancras station. Of the inclines, the most famous is perhaps Middleton, of 708 yards at 1 in 8¾, where the engine house and contents, which worked for 134 years until its retirement in 1963, have been preserved. In contrast at the Whaley Bridge end, the more shallow incline there was worked throughout by horses until 1952, due to a low bridge. Horses were favoured for hauling wagons on the level sections, although attempts were made using steam powers in the 1830s. Possibly difficulties in getting the engines to and from the flat sections of line made remote by the inclines precluded their use, though in later years they were manhandled up or down. Perhaps it is unbelievable nowadays, but passengers were carried until about 1877, the journey taking some 16 hours due to the inclines. Freight traffic included limestone, silica sand, milk and bricks as well water supplies for the system itself and for houses en route.

There was, then, a railway line of sorts in the Buxton area fulfilling the basic needs of moving limestone to where it was needed and of linking up the Midland counties with Lancashire and Cheshire. It was the Midland Railway, based in Derby, who first attempted a more positive link with their Manchester, Buxton, Matlock & Midland Junction Railway (fine initials to adorn the sides of a wagon!) which would run from Ambergate on the line to Chesterfield, westwards to join the Manchester & Birmingham Railway south of the former city. However, railway politics came into play here, as this company was later to join the London & Birmingham Railway to become the mighty LNWR who would certainly not brook any sort of competition with a rival, with the result that, having nowhere welcoming to go, the MR settled for a branch line, opened on 4th. June 1849, from Ambergate to Rowsley.

In 1846 the early form of the later Manchester, Sheffield & Lincolnshire Railway, the Sheffield, Ashton-under-Lyne & Manchester Railway, proposed a route to Whaley Bridge which soon foundered, this time because of lack of cash; work stopped in 1848 with abandonment beyond Hyde in Cheshire. The proposal is of interest, however, in that the route would have taken in Buxton.

Shed scene at Buxton in 1955, with Class 3F No. 43370, a Class 4 2-6-4T, on 8F and a Super D 0-8-0.   *The Midland Railway Trust Ltd.*

The LNWR were, meanwhile, manoeuvring on the sidelines with a view to entering Buxton, and lent their support to a further set of initials, the Stockport, Disley & Whaley Bridge Railway, a move which caused a furore among the other contenders who made efforts to ensure that the line would not enter Buxton, to which the MR and MS & L were in fact striving. Their efforts in this direction were renewed, reviving the earlier schemes and with the MR surveying a line of route from Rowsley to Buxton in 1858. By an Act of 25th. May 1860 they gained powers for a line of fifteen miles from Rowsley to Buxton, on which work began in September 1860. Not to be outdone, the LNWR cast aside any sort of gentleman's agreement over Buxton, showing support for the SD & WBR who had gained permission for an extension to Buxton on 27th. July 1857. Having gained this foothold, the LNWR now sought a lease from the C & HP to improve their line from Whaley to Buxton, and also over the Midland by proposing a through station at Buxton and a projection of the line through to Rowsley of all places; strange it is that some locations in railway history become magnetic points for various schemes. Fortunately for the MR this was not achieved. A terminal site for the MR was found in Buxton and the company began to run its passenger services from 1st. June 1863, two weeks before the LNWR which had pitched its own terminus alongside, a curious phenomenon but in the spirit of 'if one can't beat 'em join 'em'. as was indeed the fact, since a short spur connected the two premises. These structures were designed by Paxton and J. Smith and looked like identical twins from outside, though the interiors wer different in ways such as the MR windows and doors having square toplights, while those of the LNWR were semi-circular. The buildings were of red sandstone, a material unusual in the area and probably available as left-overs from the excavations for Dove Holes tunnel nearby. Euston directors must smile in their graves at the position in Buxton today, where of the two structures only the roofless LNWR version survives. Spur or no, the LNWR would not allow the MR to run through trains to or from Manchester via Stockport, so that the costly decision was made to build a separate line for Miller's Dale to New Mills where the MS & L line could be reached and the Marple, New Mills and Hayfield Junction Railway. Agreement over this was finalised on 7th. November 1861. Buxton was now virtually at the end of a 5¾ mile branch from Miller's Dale.

Here, then, were two companies, each with a branch line terminus at Buxton and of the two it was perhaps the LNWR who was the more restless and anxious to establish itself more firmly. A perpetual lease had been taken of the C & HP in 1861, and some tidying up of the rail formation had been done between Hindlow and Hurdlow in 1865. Also in 1865 the company proposed the 27 mile long Buxton, Sheffield & Liverpool Railway which would run from Disley to Sheffield and included a three mile line from Peak Forest to Chapel-en-le-Frith. This came to nothing. Likewise, there came along a Buxton, Chapel & Sheffield Railway of 1867 running to Attercliffe just east of Sheffield, also to be scotched, and then one of those interesting-sounding little ventures which fire the imagination, in this case the Sheffield & Buxton Narrow Gauge Railway of 1872, 24 miles of 3 ft. gauge line which would join the SD & WB route into Buxton. This scheme would certainly have enhanced the scenery, but, alas, it came to nought.

On Monday the 3d instant, an inquisition was held before Mr. Thomas Mander, Coroner for the Hundred of High Peak, on view of the body of James Mc. Own, (an Irishman,) who had been employed in the formation of the Cromford and High Peak Rail Road. After an investigation of five hours, it appeared, that on Saturday last, about six in the evening, the deceased was at the house of Mr. Daniel Pett, known by the sign of the Jug and Glass, at Hartington Nether Quarter, with several persons; that whilst there he was drinking ale until he became intoxicated, and then engaged in a fight with Joseph Heathcote, a labourer; that in the fight the deceased received no injury of sufficient consequence to produce his death, but that the same was occasioned by a fit of apoplexy with which the deceased was seized some time in the evening of the 3d instant; and the Jury returned their verdict,— " Died from a fit of apoplexy by the visitation of God."

Courtesy, Derbyshire County Council

Buxton was on the route of the Lancashire, Derbyshire & East Coast Railway between Macclesfield and Chesterfield, projected through the town, then parallel to the Midland as far as Miller's Dale where there would be a crossing by viaduct 270 ft. high. There were to be seven tunnels totalling four miles of obscurity. In the event, only the easy bit east of Chesterfield was ever completed.

Helped by the presence of railways in the town which had stations neatly sited close to the centre of things, Buxton steadily grew to around 10,000 and prospered on its reputation as a spa resort, one of the three chief inland watering places and, with the Bath, the only source of hot springs rising here at a constant temperature of 82° F and efficaceous for rheumatism and other unpleasant maladies. The Crescent, built by the Fifth Duke of Devonshire in 1786 and close to the stations could offer Tepid Baths at one end for 2/6d and Hot Baths at the other, with the Pump Room of 1894 in front. Near the vast Palace Hotel, built by Currey in 1868 is a rather curious and obvious domed building, the Devonshire Hospital, originally built as a private winter riding school. The dome is of 154 ft. diameter and is said to have been the largest in Europe at one time. Today the town is ommitted from the Peak Park map because of the limestone quarries which are immense.

Such splendour needed, in the eyes of the LNWR, to be given a wider audience and certainly to be enjoyed more conveniently, so that they looked southwards towards the C & HP, twisting its way towards the quarries in its own leisurely manner. An Act was proposed and authorised on 30th. July 1874 for the Buxton & High Peak Junction Railway which would connect the town by a line of five miles with the C & HP near Hurdlow, ironing out some fierce curves on the way. South of Buxton a two mile spur was constructed to meet the C & HP again at Harpurhill. Already the old line had been tidied up between Hindlow and Hurdlow, and with absorption by the LNWR of the C & HP in 1887 the stage was set for a route towards Ashbourne. Two viaducts of 15 and 13 arches were put in hand at Buxton, the first of which dominates the town to this day, and a tunnel of 514 yd. was required at Hinldow near the summit of the 1 in 60 climb out of the town 4½ miles away.

Uppermost in the middle of LNWR directors at this time was the possibility of through traffic from Euston to Buxton which up to now had managed with a change at Stockport on the Crewe-Manchester line. The MR had offered a daily through carriage from St. Pancras to Buxton, leaving London at 10.05am., in at 2.15pm., thus showing a good turn of speed, with the up service leaving at 1.25pm. but running all-stations to Derby and arriving in London at 6.05pm. Otherwise, it was all change at Miller's Dale on and off the branch. Possibly the competition thought that they could beat this performance over an extension of the line down to Hurdlow as far as Ashbourne and the end of the North Staffs. branch to Uttoxeter, which led in turn on to Burton and over the MR to Rugby. The LNWR enjoyed running powers over the NSR which could easily by invoked as well as a joint arrangement with the MR as far as Nuneaton. An Act authorised on 4th. August 1890 permitted the construction of the Ashbourne & Buxton Railway of 13 miles from the existing C & HP line at Parsley Hay to an end-on junction with the NSR at Ashbourne, to give a total mileage from Uttoxeter to Buxton of 33½ miles. Matters progressed in easy stages, with the line opened from Buxton to Hurdlow in 1892 as well as the doubling from Hindlow to Parsley Hay. In May 1893 a goods depot was opened at Higher Buxton. The line from Buxton to Parsley Hay was inspected by the Board of Trade on 29th. May 1894 and opened to passengers from 1st. June 1894. Plans for the rest of the line southwards had been ready since June 1893, but Messrs. Naylor Bros. did not start on the contract until December 1895, adding the station buildings from March 1898. Prime engineering features on the new line were the Coldeaton cutting which was 60 ft. deep and ¾ mile long, Ashbourne tunnel of 378 yd. beneath the town, and up to 40 bridges. Generally, the gradient up from Ashbourne was at 1 in 59, which ruled out bouts of heavy freight from the outset. The summit at Hindlow was 1,192 ft. Some 200 navvies and eight steam cranes were employed, with the men, a total of 500 or so, using the Ashbourne station premises prior to their opening for public use. Southwards from Parsley Hay the line, though built for double track, was only laid as single, there being however passing loops except at Thorpe Cloud. As the great man of the guide books, Baddeley, aptly said of the line: 'The route is the antitheseis of that between Dore and Chinley, being all along the tops instead of the bottoms.'

At the other end of things Ashbourne had been attempting to put itself on the railway map since the 1830s, trying, like many folk elsewhere, to bring to fruition various proposals. In 1884 an attempt had been made to provide a branch line through the town to link the Churnet Valley line near Rocester (itself a paper project) to the North Midland route at Duffield. In fact, neither the Churnet line in its original form, nor the route through Ashbourne was approved, and Churnet Valley supporters with their route from Macclesfield to Derby had to join forces with the Staffordshire Potteries Railway to form the Churnet, Potteries & Trent Valley Railway, later known as the handier sounding North Staffordshire Railway which became reality and which constructed what was to become the first NSR branch line, namely that to Ashbourne opened on 31st. May 1852, quite cheaply at about £10,000 for each mile, including a few crossings of the Dove. The contractors were Brassey & Co. and work commenced in July 1851 with a suitable celebration at the 'Green Man', Ashbourne, after which a procession with music and navvies with their wheelbarrows wound its way to Side's Mill at Clifton, where the chairman of the Ashbourne committee, Mr. Witham, cut the first sod. Afterwards the whole assembly returned to the 'Green Man' to continue the celebrations with an excellent meal 'got up at short notice' and choice wines. On the opening day too, there was more feasting at a banquet for 350 held in the goods warehouse, as the passenger station had not yet been built, while the 420 workmen had their meal in a marquee erected nearby. The bells of Ashbourne church rang and the choir of the Collegiate church of Manchester rendered 'Hail, Smiling Morn' among other selections and various back-slapping and speeches.

As mentioned, the two stations at Buxton were cheek by jowl and enjoyed no advantages one over the other as regards location; if anything, the LNWR entry and exit was superior, being higher than the Midland layout and, on leaving the terminus and sweeping round to the south over the long, high viaduct, views of the other premises and of the MR locomotive shed could be seen below. The LNWR shed was a little further out down the line towards Whaley Bridge. Just outside, the spur from the latter line came in as a sort of by-pass to the stations for non-stopping services, while a flyover line also came in from the sidings nearby. There was an easy start with a short fall, then a gentle rise up to Higher Buxton station on a level stretch. This was a simple affair with a medium sized goods yard on the right hand down side overseen by the signal box on the same side. The station lay to the south of that part called Higher Buxton; in fact the older part of the town with a onetime village green which became the market place. Here is to be found the oldest church in Buxton, dating from 1625 after the abandonment of the well chapel. More prosaic, perhaps, is the football ground nearby, as well as the cattle market on the town side. Although doubtlessly well-used, one has the feeling that Higher Buxton station was opened in order that the town might be given a stop by trains which would otherwise have sped through, avoiding the terminus, which was in fact the case for a time.

From here began the long haul, first over another viaduct across the Duke's Drive which was built to link the highways to Ashbourne and to Bakewell, upwards at 1 in 60 for 4½ miles to the summit of the line above Hurdlow, exceeded only by the run up from the other direction, for this was a cruel line for firemen. The Buxton Limes Firms Company was a group of quarry owners which registered its activities locally with the sight of excavations, processing works, much white dust and sidings along the line hereabouts, the first of these being Beswick's Sidings with its signal box on the left hand side and, opposite, the Burlow Wagon Works with a loop line giving access to a largish yard. A short distance further on and the original formation of the C & HP came in from the north west, a single line from Harpur Hill and Ladmanlow, where were a whole realm of quarry lines and workings. This innocuous line, with a 1 in 41 gradient on one short length, was operated without block or bell and was latterly virtually regarded as a long siding extension from Hindlow, which ran alongside the down side for a about one mile to the station area giving an appearance of three tracks, to reach the goods yard and shed behind the platforms. Hindlow station was the first of the typical, wooden built jobs for this line, not unattractive but with platform surfaces of wood which could be very slippery in wet weather and with buildings which tended to peel and sag gracefully with age. The old single line run of the C & HP had been coming up alongside here, rather sinuously and now did a sharp curve leftwards in best toy train tradition to cross the new route just south east of

Alsop signal box and nameboard are visible here as No. 42365 runs in with a local service. 30/10/54.   *The Midland Railway Trust Ltd.*

Location

The Tissington Trail follows the former Buxton to Ashbourne Railway Line for 13 miles between Ashbourne and Parsley Hay (Grid Ref: SK 147636). The 11½ miles from Ashbourne to Hartington opened to the public in June, 1971, and the remaining section was opened in May 1972. The High Peak Trail extends some 17½ miles along the former Cromford and High Peak Railway from Cromford to Dowlow, near Buxton. Within the National Park the High Peak Trail runs for 10½ miles from Daisy Bank near Longcliffe, to Dowlow, connecting with the Tissington Trail at Parsley Hay. Derbyshire County Council has a separate leaflet for its south-eastern section of the High Peak Trail.

Using the Trails

The Trails are fine scenic routes through varied countryside, where visitors can enjoy a picnic, long and short walks, pony trekking, cycling and nature study. It is our way of letting you see some of the National Park's unspoilt countryside, without cars, noise and other products of the 20th century getting in your way. Just relax and enjoy the Trails in your own way, but please take into consideration other people's enjoyment and observe the bye-laws.

The Trails form a central spine, and nearby walking and cycling routes are signposted, providing links to the places of interest, and circuit routes of varying lengths, from each of the car parks. (yellow and red arrows are the waymarks for walking and cycling routes, respectively, described in the White Peak 'Routes for People' leaflets. The walks leaflet is available free from signboard dispensers at various car parks in the area, and the priced cycling leaflet is available from Information Centres and the National Park Office). Cycles may be hired during the summer from Parsley Hay, and Middleton Top on the High Peak Trail and from Station Road, Ashbourne. Details can be obtained from the National Park Office at Bakewell, or from Information Centres.

The Youth and Schools Liaison Service can provide information and advice on the educational use of the Trails. Write to: Losehill Hall, Castleton, Derbyshire S30 2WB. Telephone: Hope Valley (0433) 20373.

How to get there

There are daily bus services between Buxton and Hartington, and services on market days and Saturdays between Ashbourne and Hartington. In addition, special summer Sunday and Bank Holiday Monday services run between Buxton and Ashbourne, with through buses or connections to Derby, Chesterfield, Sheffield, the Potteries and Manchester.

A priced series of timetable leaflets with details of all public transport facilities in the National Park is available from Centres and the National Park Office. Separate leaflets for services in the Manifold Valley, Dovedale and the Tissington Trail can also be obtained from National Park Information Centres.

The following coach operators provide local services in the vicinity of the trail and for up-to-date details of timetables, visitors are advised to contact the Companies direct:

D. Glover, 56 Walton Crescent, Ashbourne (Ashbourne2788)

W. N. Warrington, The Cottage, Ilam, Nr. Ashbourne (Thorpe Cloud 204)

H. Hulley & Sons Ltd., Baslow, Nr. Bakewell (Baslow 2246)

B. L. Sutton, Hillview, Reapsmoor, Longnor, Nr. Buxton (Hartington 211)

Trent Motor Traction Co. Ltd., Uttoxeter New Road, Derby (Derby 4320)

Berresfords Coaches, Cheddleton, Nr. Leek (Stoke 560240)

15

the station and over the mouth of the tunnel. With a secondary road now running due north-south beneath the two lines, this left a neat triangle in which was built a large quarry with its attendant works and chimneys neatly obscuring the skyline. Sidings were put in here to serve the premises concerned. Originally Hindlow was a hamlet of barely half a dozen houses when the railway arrived, with one siding off the C & HP. Little justified the existence of the LNWR station here, with nothing but the A515 road half a mile to the north and plenty of tumuli. The later quarries would generate more in the way of passenger traffic.

At a point south of the tunnel the old, disused C & HP formation came in from the north side, crossed and then fell in with the new alignment, the two being as one form here to Parsley Hay. At Briggs Sidings, 1 mile 396 yd. from Hindlow, and at Dowlow Halt, 423 yd. further on, two more spurs went off from the down side, to run as far as the steep Edges to serve quarries. The halt here, opened in 1917, would serve the local quarry workers, since road access was nil. A rather precipitous run downhill now, to the next station of Hurdlow at 2 miles 213 yd., through countryside which is hardly featureless, but bare and bleak. Hurdlow as a village does not exist, only a name on the map, though next to the station was Sparklow, a small hamlet on the down side with, however, the 'Royal Oak' public house handily placed. The road to Monyash, a large village two miles away to the east crossed the line by a bridge, while the station, devoid of any goods yard except one siding, but with a crossover and signal box on the east side, lay waiting for the point-to-point races at Flagg on Easter Tuesday each year. Rather significantly, perhaps, Hurdlow closed before the others, on 15th. August 1949.

The line now became more sinuous, though less steep, turning south, then south east and south again passing odd, abandoned meanders of the earlier line to reach Parsley Hay station at 2 miles 250 yd. from Hurdlow, still high at 1,100 ft. and next to the Buxton-Ashbourne road which was a saving grace as, once more there was nothing of note to serve roundabout. The name was presumably taken from Parsley Hay farm to the north, and the station position corresponded to that of the original C & HP version. On the up side a goods line followed the formation of the first layout rather awkwardly round the curve, with two sidings off into the yard by the road, this before the station was reached and a minor road underbridge. The signal box was on the platform on the eastern side. A few yards south of the station the C & HP line left the realignment to pursue its old meandering way south east towards Cromford, the first point of importance being Friden, home to the Derbyshire Silica Firebeck Company and Blakemore Sidings.

The section of line from Buxton to Parsley Hay was opened in June 1894.

Parsley Hay marked a stage on the Ashbourne to Buxton route, as the line became single southwards, though there was provision for double track. Where the two single lines diverged, opportunity was taken to install a rather fine scissors crossing. While engineer's progress had been relatively plain sailing up to now, with only the straightening of the C & HP to worry about, things now became acutely different, with an initial half mile of limestone to be blasted away using gelignite and creating a cutting of 60 ft. in depth. On leaving the cutting, at 1,060 yd. from Parsley Hay, a short line ran off westwards to Messrs. Wragg & Sons High Peak Silica Company's quarry, given a note in the 1916 Working Appendix as follows:

'Wragg's Sidings to and from the Main Line are connected by a key attached to the train staff. Down trains from Ashbourne to Parsley Hay must stop at this Siding to attach or detach. All wagons should instead be worked to Parsley Hay and returned by an Up train. Drivers intending to use the Siding must clear the points at the Parsley Hay end of the Siding. The Goods Guard will be responsible for opening the gate as they go into the Siding and securing it on leaving to prevent cattle straying on the line.'

At Hand Dale viaduct site workmen uncovered some old mine workings containing the skeletons of trapped men. Just over Hand Dale viaduct lay Hartington station, at 3 miles 610 yd. from Parsley Hay, which could be considered as a more through-going affair than some, with a passing loop,

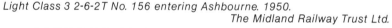

Light Class 3 2-6-2T No. 156 entering Ashbourne. 1950.
The Midland Railway Trust Ltd.

Ashbourne station looking north.   *Douglas Thompson*

Ashbourne station looking south.   *Douglas Thompson*

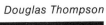

again with its signal box on the platform on the east side with goods yard adjacent, from which a long siding led into the station quarry, all of it very compact. The station nameboard 'Hartington, for Dovedale and Beresforddale', was something of a confidence trick to all but a stout rambler, as the village lay a good mile west down a steep hill and the dales were half a mile beyond that. Hartington village, styled by some the Capital of Dovedale, enjoys the distinction of a town charter going back to 1204, with a population of around 400 living in stone walled houses. Hartington Hall, now a Youth Hostel, was, from 1611, home of the Bateman family, one descendant of which became Lord Mayor of London. Isaac Walton, the 'compleat angler', did his fishing in Beresford Dale, accompanied by his companion Charles Cotton. One dale here which the line might have advertised was Wolfcote nearby.

Around Hartington the line was level, but soon began to twist and turn and climb again steadily to Alsop Moor Siding at 3 miles 932 yd. where was the brickworks of Messrs. Hall & Boardman on the up side, the siding trailing in southwards. The Appendix reads:

'The tumbler points for the sidings to the works are padlocked, and a key is in the possession of the Buxton Lime Works foreman. Trains to Ashbourne are not to call at the Siding, but wagons are to be worked to Hartington and back to the Siding by the first available service.'

Another feature of the line, Coldeaton cutting, was to be found on this section. At this point 200 men with eight steam cranes were at work at one time, removing 314 cubic yards of limestone.

The main road crossed over the line on a skew overbridge as it swept into the station at Alsop-en-la-Dale, close now to the Dove and the Staffordshire border. (1 mile 333 yd.) Again, the layout was simple, with a passing loop which was later removed, and the signal box on the platform on the west side, along with a single siding. The buildings were long, low, wooden without the benefit of awnings. Alsop village lay a short distance to the east downhill, reached quite easily by footpath. It consisted of a dozen houses or so round the church of St. Michael. The Alsop family were lords of the manor here for many years until 1880, the family name becoming very well known due to brewing interests at Burton-on-Trent. Alsop's station nameboard also carried the words 'for Alstonfield', a village about two miles away to the west.

Baddeley's guide book mentions that, in October 1889 the Duke of Devonshire cut the first sod of a light railway which would link the area around Hartington with Caldon and Leek in Staff. One wonders how far the plan went.

'Drivers of up or down trains must open the whistle when approaching the level crossing between Alsop and Tissington.' Not an unusual feature on many lines, but this was probably the only one in this case, hence the cautionary note. Still downhill, often quite steeply and with a pronounced curve the line reached Tissington station at 2 miles 1312 yd. from Alsop, a place which actually managed to be in the village it served, with passing loop, signal box on the platform and siding on the village side. Speed through the loop here was restricted to ten miles per hour in both directions. The stations here and at Hartington both had awnings, giving a more satisfactory effect and being practical.

If Hartington could be known as the capital of Dovedale, then Tissington, lying away from all the splendour, had to be Derbyshire's prettiest village,

L M S
LONDON MIDLAND AND SCOTTISH RAILWAY

HALF-DAY TRIP
TO
DOVEDALE

On SUNDAY, August 17, 1930
AN HALF-DAY EXCURSION
WILL BE RUN AS UNDER
TO

Ashbourne, Thorpe Cloud, Alsop-en-le-Dale and BUXTON

FROM	Starting Times	RETURN FARES 3rd Class			
		Ashbourne	Thorpe Cloud	Alsop-en-le-Dale	Buxton
Birmingham (New Street)					
Vauxhall					
Aston					
Gravelly Hill					
Erdington					
Chester Road					
Sutton Coldfield					
Four Oaks					
WOLVERHAMPTON (H.L.)					
Willenhall (Bilston Street)					
Darlaston					
Walsall					
Pelsall					
Brownhills					
Hammerwich					
Hednesford					
Cannock					
Wyrley and C.H.					
Bloxwich					
Lichfield City					
Arrival Times		12 40	12 51	11	50

Conditions of Issue of Excursion
and other Reduced Fare Tickets.
Excursion Tickets, and Tickets issued at Fares less than the Ordinary Fares, are issued
subject to the Notices and Conditions shewn in the Company's current Time Tables.

PLEASE RETAIN THIS BILL FOR REFERENCE.

(200—18,000) McCorquodale & Co. Ltd., Printers, London and New York.—1227   [See Over.

RETURN ARRANGEMENTS.

Passengers return the same day from Burton ... Alsop-en-le-Dale ... ...
0.0 p.m. Ashbourne 9.20 p.m. ... ...

The ideal way of seeing the beauties of Dovedale is to enter the Dale in the vicinity of Thorpe Cloud Station, and walk through, emerging in the district of Alsop-en-le-Dale Station, or vice versa. Passengers holding Alsop-en-le-Dale Tickets are allowed to alight or join the train at Thorpe Cloud Station.

Day and Period Excursion Tickets can be obtained in advance from Adderley Park, Aston, Bournville, Brighton Road, Camp Hill, Chester Road, Erdington, Five Ways, Gravelly Hill, Great Barr, Hagley Road, Harborne, Hazelwell, Icknield Port Road, King's Heath, Lifford, Monument Lane, Moseley, Perry Barr, Rotton Park, Saltley, Selly Oak, Soho Road, Stechford, Vauxhall, Witton Green, And Witton Stations, available from and to Birmingham only. Period Tickets from Foleshill, available from and to Coventry only, and Period Tickets from Bloxwich, available from and to Walsall only.

Tickets and Small Bills can be obtained at the Stations and from the following Excursion Offices in BIRMINGHAM: 46, Snow Hill; 1, George Street Parade; 44, Hall Street; 2, Edgbaston Street; Enquiry Office, New Street Station (next Queen's Hotel), Tel. 2740 Mid., Extension 18 or 41; also from L.M.S. Railway ...

Messrs. THOS. COOK & SON, LTD.—

Birmingham—Stephenson Place, Tel. 4357 Midland, ...
... ... 52 & 54, Corporation St., Tel. 4089 Central.
Wolverhampton—22, Lichfield Street, Tel. ... ...

Messrs. W. H. HAYWARD & SON—
Birmingham—41, Union Passage, Tel. ... Mid.

TRAVELLERS LTD. (British and Irish Travel Agency)
Birmingham—43, Temple Row, Tel. 3939/33 Central.

Messrs. J. JOHNSON & CO., LTD.—
Birmingham—32, Paradise Street, Tel. 3671 Mid.

Messrs. PICKFORD'S, LTD.—
Birmingham—573, Moseley Road, Tel. South 918.
... ... 105, Alum Rock Road, Saltley, Tel. East 178.
... ... 147, Corporation Street, Tel. Cen. 1850/1158.

Mr. W. H. GAZELEY—
Dudley—101, Castle Street, ...
Brierley Hill—131, High Street.
Walsall—12, Park Street, Tel. 3931.
West Bromwich—41, High Street, ...
Wolverhampton—... ... Princes Square.
Birmingham—53, Snow Hill, Tel. ... ...
... ... Corporation Street ... 10688 Central.
Erdington—... ... ... 435 ...

Kidderminster—... ... ...

BIRMINGHAM CO-OPERATIVE SOCIETY, LTD.—
Birmingham—Travel House, 19, Ashted Row, ... 1901/2.

Small Bills can also be obtained at the Company's ... ... Offices.

FIRST AND THIRD CLASS WEEK-END TICKETS.

These Tickets will be issued at any Station on the London Midland and Scottish Railway to any other Station in Great Britain, and Ports and Inland Stations in Ireland (where through Fares are in operation) by any train at a Single Fare and a Third for the Double Journey (fractional part of 3d. reckoned as 3d.). Where there are no Through Fares in operation, arrangements will be made for the issue of Week-end Tickets upon 48 hours notice being given at the Station from which the journey will be commenced.

	OUTWARD	RETURN	MINIMUM FARES.
	By any train on	By any train on	
FRIDAYS at or after 4.0 a.m.	Following Saturday, Sunday, Monday		
SATURDAYS	Same day or following Sunday, Monday		
SUNDAYS	Same day or following Monday, Tuesday		

WORKS' OUTINGS, PICNICS, CHOIR PARTIES, &c.

Special arrangements and facilities can be made for ... on convenient ... Works Outings, including Workpeople's Excursions, Choir Outings, Pleasure Parties, Picnics, &c. Secretaries are invited to make their arrangements early, and are requested to apply to ... Stations and Agencies, or communicate with the Divisional Passenger Commercial Superintendent, New Street Station, Birmingham.

Tickets can be obtained in advance from the Station Booking Offices and Agencies.

Children under 3 years of age free, and under 14 half-fare.

LUGGAGE ARRANGEMENTS.

Day and Half-day Excursion Tickets—Passengers holding day or half-day ... tickets by special trains are not allowed to take any luggage except small hand articles intended for the use of the passenger, and during the day ... ... only, ... may take with them free of charge ... ...

Passengers holding Period Excursion Tickets are allowed ... ... holding 100 lbs. in weight, and in order that this may be ... it is essential that all ... be removed or defaced and that the packages be fully and legibly ... ... of the luggage, when a full name and address should be placed in each package.

All information regarding Excursion Trains on the London Midland and Scottish Railway may be obtained on application to L.M.S. Stations and Agencies, or to the Divisional Passenger Commercial Superintendent, New Street Station, Birmingham.

July, 1930.

FOLLOWS,
Vice-President.

being approached along the road through an avenue of lime trees. Here was the home of the Fitzherbert family, of whom Alleyne became this country's ambassador, first in Brussels, then in Russia at the time of Catherine the Great. It is, however, for the well dressings that Tissington is famous, a ritual which has proceeded from pagan times as gratitude to the gods for the provision of much needed water which was especially appreciated in an area of porous limestone. On and after Ascension Day each year five wells around the village, the Hands, Hall, Town, Yew Tree and Coffin were elaborately decked with flowers to propitiate the divine powers, all of which no doubt added to the revenue at Tissington station. Signalman Walker here was an actual well-dresser in the village.

From here is the steepest gradient, a long descent at 1 in 59 right down into Ashbourne, the line first passing the siding at Fenny Bentley (1,373 yd.) near a skew overbridge across the main road. It was obviously not worth establishing a station here, as the small village lay astride the main road to the south. Its houses were now of brick as the soil turned redder as the Peak Park was left behind. Beresford Old Hall has become Cherry Orchard Farm, and of the Beresfords one of the family, Thomas, is worthy of note as a doughty survivor of Agincourt who was buried in the church in 1473 with his wife and 23 children.

'Down goods trains from Ashbourne having wagons to attach or detach at Fenny Bentley must not have more than eighteen wagons including the brake. Under no circumstances must wagons be brought out on to the main line without the engine at the Ashbourne end of them, except when the train is right away.'

After Fenny Bentley came the station at Thorpe Cloud (1,083 yd.), really little more than a halt; nevertheless it had a porter in charge and a sort of goods loop-cum-siding at the Ashbourne end on the west side. The outfit was released by a key attached to the train staff. The station site was set on a curve, with the platform on the west side. Thorpe village exists and lay half a mile west of the station, with the Dove a further half mile west of that, all carefully programmed for the rambler, one might surmise, especially with the Peveril Hotel en route and the Isaac Walton Hotel at the end of the walk over the bridge, beyond which lay Ilam. Beauty is in abundance here at the spot where the Manifold joins the Dove. The two prominent heights are Bunster, over on the Staffordshire side of the dale, 1,000 ft., and Thorpe Cloud, 942 ft. which is conical in shape. Linguists may ponder the fact that 'thorpe' is a Danish name in a Saxon area, while 'clud' is an old English word for 'rock' or 'hill'. 'Thorpe Cloud' made an attractive name for a railway station, avoided confusion with Thorpes elsewhere and brought in the adventurous with their rucksacks and tents.

Crossing a seven arch viaduct en route, the long steep gradient persisted all the way down into Ashbourne station, at 2 miles 1,359 yd., road and railway never far apart in pleasant, rolling countryside without any clusters of habitation to justify another station. The river, too, was off away to the west and had lost the closeness of its dale. Although the line here was steep, banking engines were not permitted up to Parsley Hay from Ashbourne, probably because of the single line. However, they were permitted both from Buxton and from Parsley Hay up to Brigg's Sidings at the northern, double tracked end. Single line tokens were used as follows:

Parsley Hay-Hartington	Blue.
Hartington-Alsop	Red.
Alsop-Tissington	Blue.
Tissington-Ashbourne No. 2	Red.
Parsley Hay-Friden	Round blue.

Hindlow, looking towards the tunnel.   *Douglas Thompson*

A rule stated that all goods trains should have 20 ton brake vans, also that all goods trains should stop at Brigg's Sidings starting signal to apply the side brakes on wagons, these to be released on the arches between Higher Buxton and Buxton No. 2 signal boxes. Likewise, from Parsley Hay to Ashbourne, trains were to stop at Bridge No. 14 to apply the wagon brakes which could not be released until Ashbourne No. 2 starting signal.

The long, low station building at Alsop-en-le-Dale.   *Douglas Thompson*

Ashbourne gained a mention in the Domesday Book as Erseburne or similar, in the way in which early place names varied. It is an active, rather diffident little town in the fertile valley of the Henmore Brook, over a mile away from the Dove to its west, protected by hills on three sides, but with good views over the valley southwards. During the Civil War Charles I visited the Parish church and fought two battles here, that in 1644 when he was defeated, and the second one year later, when he was victorious. St. Oswald's was consecrated in 1241 and contains memorials to three local families, the Cockaynes, the Boothbys and the Bradbournes. Apart from Royalty, the most eminent visitor was Dr. Johnson, who visited his friend, the Rev. Dr. Taylor who resided in the house which found itself near the railway station and so gave passengers waiting on the platform chance to enjoy the view of its pleasant garden. The wife of the Salvationist General Booth, Catherine, was a native of the town. In 1896 the township had 3,868 inhabitants, rising to 5,440 in 1951. The town is well connected by its roads to the outside world; no less than six radiate out to Buxton, Bakewell, Belper, Leek, Lichfield and Derby, whereas the railway system could only manage an initial branch up from Uttoxeter in 1852, which remained the sole connection until the LNWR came down from Buxton almost fifty years later.

The North Staffordshire Railway provided a small terminus a few yards to the south west of the final joint station just west of where the footbridge ran. This latter was formerly the roadway in front of the premises, later Old Station road which was truncated to allow the lines to be extended through. A small yard was provided, with goods depot and small engine shed on the south side. When it was decided to provide a through station, the yard was left here and extended slightly, while the station was sited on a curve turning northwards to burrow under Church st. by a tunnel of 390 yd. The platforms were given a bay each at the Uttoxter end and the buildings were of the standard wooden pattern found elsewhere on the LNWR branch. An LNWR pattern signal box was sited on the outside of the curve to the rear of the platform, while the NSR cabin was rebuilt in the same position and worked the goods side of things.

Later on, the Nestlé Company added their condensed milk factory with its siding to the yard not far from the two road engine shed, while nearby was a cheese factory which was unconnected to rail. The original Railway Hotel hostelry, the Station Hotel, was built opposite to the new premises served by a new roadway from Church street. Other items nearby were the football ground, a cinema and a corset factory.

Building the viaduct at Hand Dale. The crane is in a precarious position.

National Railway Museum

As eventually happened, the line which we are dealing with, and the branch to Uttoxeter were taken as part of one length for operating purposes, running from Edgeley Junction at Stockport. We shall therefore exercise a compromise and take the North Staffs. branch as far as the Staffs. border, leaving Ashbourne and running south west to Clifton for Mayfield station at 1½ miles, which was a more substantial affair than the LNWR had provided so far, with neat parallel platforms and a brick building on the west side at the north end by the level crossing (for a change), supervised by the signal box. On the west side was a small goods yard and a long siding to Simpson's Mayfield Cotton Mill, situated in the village of Church Mayfield. Clifton village lay close by on the other side of the line. South of the station the running lines became single, the convergence and yard exit supervised by another, smaller cabin. Norbury & Ellaston, the next station (2¾ miles) had a passing loop with parallel platforms and signal box on the west side along with the centrally placed station building. There was a siding on the east side. The local corn mills lay nearby, but were not linked to the line. Norbury is a tiny village whose cottages lie on the bank of the Dove with a Norman church and manor house which belonged to the Fitzherbert family of Tissington. Ellaston lies across the river and does not have much on ready offer.

The single line continued on its way to Rocester (2½ miles) and out of the scrutiny of this little book.

A rather jolly happening for the line was that, before public services ran, a free excursion was offered for the folf of Hartington to visit Ashbourne as an 'opener', no doubt showing the importance of potential custom in the village, or was it due to the influence of some benign local worthy?

Passenger workings on the line were basically for local travellers, though some services did originate from as far as Manchester in the early days, just as there were odd connections with NSR trains to Uttoxeter. There were 7-8 trains each way daily, two of these conveying the London through coach in each direction.

Passenger services in July 1902 were as follows:

Manchester:	"	"	"	10.15am SO	"	"	"	"
Stockport:	"	"	"	10.25	"	"	"	"
Buxton: 8.05am	8.50	10.30		11.08h	1.20pm*	2.30	5.50	7.15 SO
Ashbourne: 8.48	9.44	11.30		12.06	2.05	3.30	7.00	8.15

* Runs express to Hartington. Conveys through coach. h Stops at Higher Buxton, not terminus.

Ashbourne: 7.30am	10.50	2.35pmx	4.15		5.35	7.30v	7.10	9.27x
Buxton: 8.55	11.50	3.20	5.10		6.35	8.25	8.10	10.12
Stockport:	"	"	"		"	9.09	"	"
Manchester:	"	"	"		"	9.25	"	"

Super D 0-8-0 No. 49210 brings a down freight train through Ashbourne station. 26/6/59.   *The Midland Railway Trust Ltd.*

x Runs express from Hartington with through coach. v Does not call at Hindlow or Hurdlow and calls Higher Buxton as timed, not at terminus. No Sunday service.

The through carriages were timed as follows:

Buxton:	8.05am	1.20pm*		Euston:	11.00am*	5.35pm
Ashbourne:	8.50	2.07		Numeaton: (slip)s	1.08pm	8.00
Uttoxeter arr:	9.12	2.33		Burton arr:	1.45	8.35
dep:	9.17	2.40		dep:	1.48	8.38
Burton arr:	9.40	3.03		Uttoxeter arr:	2.10	9.00
dep:	9.45	3.08		dep:	2.15	9.05
Nuneaton:	10.28	3.48		Ashbourne arr:	2.33	9.25
Euston arr:	1.05pm	6.00		dep:	2.35	9.27
				Buxton:	3.20	10.12

* Calls at Clifton, Norbury, Rocester and Tutbury to take up for London if a signal is given, or to set down Londond passengers if necessary.

The service was discontinued at some time during the Great War, probably in 1917, not to be resumed. Although quicker than by way of Stockport, the routeing was somewhat recondite and could not really have been developed over the lines as they stood.

In 1914 the pattern was as below, with the two London throughs each way and a somewhat different set of departures. A Sunday service had appeared:

Up. Weekdays.

Manchester London Rd:	"	7.35	"	1.00pm SX	"
Buxton:	7.30am h	10.30	12.45pm	2.30	5.55
Ashbourne:	8.29	11.30	1.31	3.25	7.00
London Euston arr:	12.30pm	"	5.41*	"	"

Sundays

Manchester London Rd:	"	"	"	"	"
Buxton:	5.00pm h	"	"	"	"
Ashbourne:	6.15	"	"	"	"

h not Higher Buxton. * Express to Hartington.

Down. Weekdays.

London Euston dep:	"	"	10.37*	"	"	5.30*h
Buxton:	8.12	11.52	3.40	5.19	8.57	10.15

Sundays

London Euston dep:	"	"	"	"	"	"
Ashbourne:	7.15pm	"	"	"	"	"
Buxton:	8.15	"	"	"	"	"

* Express from Huntington. h not Higher Buxton.

At this time it might be of interest to mention that the Midland could offer a departure from London St. Pancras at 10.05am which arrived in Buxton at the adjacent station at 2.28pm., while a return trip left at 5.35pm., getting back into London at 9.45pm. This did in fact undercut the LNWR timing over the new route by over half an hour.

Work in progress on Ashbourne tunnel. The foreman in centre stage in classic pose. National Railway Museum

THORPE CLOUD   CTG

In 1925, following Grouping, the LMS provided the following, still with a Sunday service to cater for the churchgoers in all probability. The local to Hartington is interesting:

Up. Weekdays.

Buxton: 7.10am 10.02SO 10.33　　1.25pmSO 1.45SX 2.40SO 5.50　7.50SOx
Ashbourne: 8.37w　10.28h　11.31　　2.26　　　2.46　　3.40　　7.05　9.00

Sundays.

Buxton: 4.48pm　　"　　　"　　　"　　　"　　　"　　　"　　　"
Ashbourne: 5.56　　"　　　"　　　"　　　"　　　"　　　"　　　"

w waits 15 minutes at Parsley Hay. h starts at Hartington.
x not Higher Buxton.

Down. Weekdays.

Ashbourne: 7.45am　9.15SO 11.05　　1.24SO　　1.45SO 4.10　　7.50　9.15SO
Buxton: 8.56　　9.48h　12.20pm 2.26　　2.46　　5.21　　9.00 10.00x

Sundays.

Ashbourne: 7.20pm　　"　　　"　　　"　　　"　　　"　　　"　　　"
Buxton: 8.05x　　"　　　"　　　"　　　"　　　"　　　"　　　"

h arrives Hartington. x not Higher Buxton.

In 1938, perhaps a highpoint for passenger workings on the line, the following was to be found:

Up. Weekdays.

Buxton:　　7.07am　　9.15SO　10.35　　　1.45pmSX　1.55SO
Ashbourne:　8.39x　　10.11　　11.34*　　2.41　　　2.51
Buxton:　　3.15SO　　6.10aSO　5.55SX　　6.00SO　　7.50SO
Ashbourne:　4.11　　6.26　　6.53*　　7.00*　　8.47h

x waits 28 minutes at Parsley Hay. * to Uttoxter. h not Higher Buxton.
a from Alsop.

30

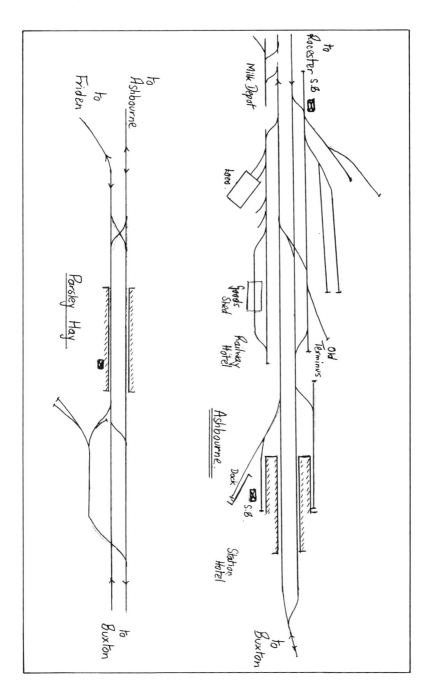

to
Rocester S.B.

Milk Depot

Shed.

Goods
Shed

Railway
Hotel

Ashbourne.

to
Ashbourne

to
Friden

Parsley Hay

Old
Terminus

Dock

S.B.

Station
Hotel

to
Buxton

to
Buxton

Down. Weekdays.

Ashbourne:	7.50am	10.28	11.08SO	4.18	5.40a
Buxton:	8.53	11.28*	12.19pm	5.20	6.01
Ashbourne:	7.10hhSO	7.50	9.15SO	''	''
Buxton:	8.06	8.47	10.12h	''	''

* from Uttoxeter. a to Alsop. hh not Hurdlow or Higher Buxton.
h not Higher Buxton.

An impressive set of services had also been put forward for Sundays:

Buxton:	10.30am	1.35pm	4.48*	7.50r	''
Ashbourne:	11.18	2.29	5.55	8.48	''
Ashbourne:	12.00pm	3.30r	7.05*	''	''
Buxton:	12.58	4.15	8.03	''	''

* to or from Uttoxeter. r to or from Rocester.

By wartime, in 1942, the following applied, with a long morning wait for breakfast at Parsley Hay, and still with the short trip between Alsop and Ashbourne. The Sunday service had disappeared.

Up.

| Buxton: | 7.07am | 10.35 | 2.05pmSO | 5.55 | '' |
| Ashbourne: | 8.32x | 11.34 | 2.21a | 6.53 | '' |

x waits 27 minutes at Parsley Hay. a from Alsop.

| Ashbourne: | 7.50am | 10.38SX | 11.08SO | 1.35SO | 4.18 |
| Buxton: | 8.53 | 11.39 | 12.19pm | 1.56a | 5.20 |

a to Alsop.

Near the end of passenger workings things were reduced to three trains each way daily, and these were worked through to and from Uttoxeter. In December 1951 the following applied:

Up.

Buxton:	7.07am	10.25	5.55pmSX	6.20SO
Ashbourne:	8.30	11.18	6.50	7.15
Ashbourne:	8.47	11.22	6.55	7.20
Uttoxeter:	9.12x	11.47	7.27	7.52

Down.

Uttoxeter:	10.15am	''	3.45pmSX	3.55SO
Ashbourne:	10.42	''	4.11	4.21
Ashbourne:	10.52	7.50am	4.18	4.25
Buxton:	11.53	8.50	5.17	5.22

x waits 31 minutes at Parsley Hay.
Higher Buxton and Hurdlow stations had closed.

The passenger service ceased on 1st. November 1954, trains having for many years been worked by a tank engine and two coaches. There were some excursions and emergency services which were seen until 7th. October 1963. The Rocester-Ashbourne branch of the NSR lost its passenger trains at the same time, since it was considered as part of the run to Buxton. Total closure followed on 1st. June 1964.

An excursion train enters Ashbourne from the south, headed by No. 42668 on 18/5/59.   *The Midland Railway Trust Ltd.*

Having again mentioned the NSR branch, reference should be made to the developments here, with the Churnet Valley line crossing along first, opening between North Rode and Uttoxeter in July 1849. The branch to Ashbourne was authorised on 22nd. July 1848 and opened on 31st. May 1852. In 1881 Uttoxeter gained a triangular layout when a new north-west curve was laid in, enabling Stoke trains to reach Ashbourne and the Churnet Valley line without reversal. The latter line closed in 1960, though there were Leek-Uttoxeter workmen's services up to 1965.

It was stipulated that all local passenger and goods services working between Parsley Hay and Ashbourne should be worked by tank engines and should stop at each station. This was adhered to, except in the case of through trains which were permitted the use of tender locomotives, providing that the engine was first. Procedures for dealing with wagons at sidings controlled by ground frames en route have been mentioned, the chief factor being to have the engine at the downhill end of any movement and not to have loose wagons out on the running lines.

For the freight workings, old LNWR 0-8-0s of Class 7F (or 2-8-0s of 8F) based at Buxton, a subshed of Longsight, and latterly coded 9L, were used. The LNWR engines were known to the men as 'Super Ds'. Trains of thirty wagons loaded with limestone or firebricks would halt at the top of the gradient down to Ashbourne in the Up direction for the wagon brakes to be applied. First, the guard would walk down to the engine, having left the

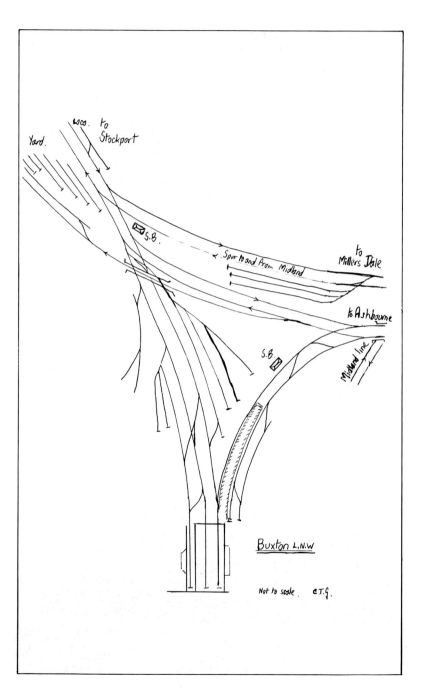

Yard.

Loco. to Stockport

S.B.

Spur to and from Midland

to Millers Dale

to Ashbourne

S.B.

Midland line.

Buxton L.N.W

Not to scale.   C.T.G.

34

handbrake van 'off'. When the guard was ready, the driver would move the train slowly and the guard would pin down the wagon brakes, using a brake stick. When the driver felt that sufficient brakes were down to give him control of the train he would whistle, and the guard would rejoin the train. The brake in the brake van would be used as reserve to control the train; it would not be used solely, as 'snatching' might result which could cause couplings to snap. The author remembers seeing an LNER Q6 0-8-0 passing him fairly briskly downhill with a loaded train of private owner coal wagons minus brake van, which followed soon afterwards in the same direction with a couple of wagons forming the short end of the train which had obviously suffered a broken wagon coupling through 'snatching'. The two parts must have been quietly reunited, as nothing further was literally heard. Care was also taken not to apply brakes too strongly, causing wheels to lock and so skid and eventually form flats on the tyres. Going northwards brakes on wagons were pinned down at Brigg's Sidings starting signal and released on the viaduct between Higher Buxton and Buxton No. 2 signal box.

No. 42667 enters Alsop-en-le-Dale station with the 10.25am from Buxton. 30/10/54. *The Midland Railway Trust Ltd.*

A typical day's freight operation is shown below from the Working Timetable for September 1953:

Up. Weekdays.

Class	Time	From	To	arr.
K	7.15am	Buxton	Brigg's Siding	7.40am
J empties	7.30SO	Buxton	Tissington	9.30

Sad scene at Ashbourne as No. 42160 waits with a track-lifting train. 9/64.   *The Midland Railway Trust Ltd.*

J empties	7.40	Buxton	Harpur Hill	8.16
G light engine	8.14*	Rowsley	Parsley Hay	8.56
				(* pass Buxton)
K	8.50	Harpur Hill	Hindlow	9.00
J empties SX	8.50	Buxton	Friden	10.05
				(Parsley Hay)
K pick-up	9.10	Buxton	Dovefields Sidings	1.54pm
				(Ashbourne)
J SO	12.10pm	Parsley Hay	Middleton Top	
K	2.00	Buxton	Ashbourne	5.07
K	3.00	Buxton	Harpur Hill	3.20
K SO	4.10	Hindlow	Brigg's Siding	

An enthusiasts' special in the form of a GWR railcar, halts at Tissington. A good display of staff and passengers is evident.   Collection C.T. Goode

K SO	4.20	Buxton	Parsley Hay	6.05	
K	5.20	Buxton	Parsley Hay	6.35	
K SO	7.00	Buxton	Brigg's Siding	7.50	
H SO	8.26	Stockport (dep. 5.29)	Brigg's Siding	9.15	
H SO	8.54	Stockport (dep. 6.46)	Brigg's Siding	9.35	

Down. Weekdays.

G	7.45am	Brigg's Siding	Buxton	8.00	
K	8.00	Brigg's Siding	Old Harpur	8.50	
G	10.15	Parsley Hay	Rowsley	11.03 (pass Buxton)	
J SO	9.05	Middleton Top	Parsley Hay	11.50	
J SX	1.35pm	Friden	Buxton	3.15	
K pickup (?)	11.40am*	Pinfold Sidings	Buxton	4.32 (*at Ashbourne)	
K	5.35pm	Ashbourne	Buxton	8.15x	

x On Saturdays engine off 4.20pm ex Buxton is coupled on at Hartington.

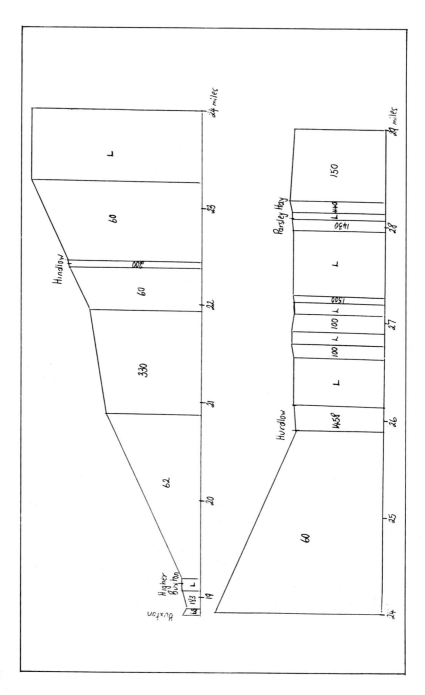

38

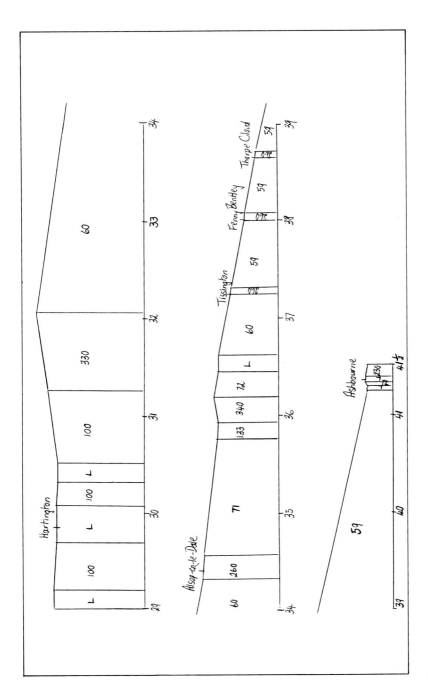

Hartington

29   30   31   32   33   34

L   100   L   100   L   100   330   60

Alsop-en-le-Dale

34   35   36   37   38   39

60   260   71   133   340   72   L   60   260   59   440   59   440   59

Tissington   Fenny Bentley   Thorpe Cloud

Ashbourne

39   40   41   41½

59   430

39

| | Ge | 8.15 | Brigg's Siding | Buxton | 8.40 |

Ge   8.15   Brigg's Siding   Buxton   8.40

e Engine and brake van off 7pm ex Buxton.

G SOv   9.25   Brigg's Siding   Buxton   9.45
          (9.50 SX)   (10.10 SX)

v After working 5.29pm (6.46 SX) from Stockport.

South of Ashbourne. Weekdays.

Class	Time	From	To	arr.
	12.20pm	Ashbourne No.1	Pinfold Sidings	1.56pm (Uttoxeter)
	1.54	Ashbourne No.1	Dovefield Sidings	2.50 (Uttoxeter)
	7.10SX*	Ashbourne No.1	Dovefield Sidings	7.58 (Uttoxeter)
	7.31SO*	Ashbourne No.1	Dovefield Sidings	8.08 (Uttoxeter)

* Worked by engine off 6.17pm. Class B from Uttoxeter.

| | 6.05am* | Pinfold Sidings | Ashbourne | 6.41am |
| | 8.38*a | Pinfold Sidings | Ashbourne | 11.40 (forward to Buxton) |

Class 7F 0-8-0 No. 49214 enters Ashbourne station with a goods train from Buxton. 1955.   *The Midland Railway Trust Ltd.*

No. 42667 at Norbury station with the 1.20pm from Uttoxeter. 30/10/54.
The Midland Railway Trust Ltd.

1.00pm	Pinfold Sidings Ashbourne		2.16pma	
SX*				

a Engine works 4.05pm Class B to Rocester. Stops at MOF Tea Siding when required. * Times at Uttoxeter.   a Conveys livestock for Rocester.

Sundays

F Milk empties	11.00am	Ashbourne	Uttoxeter	11.35am
Livestock/ Milk	9.30am	Uttoxeter	Ashbourne	10.38am

Nowadays, the section of line from Buxton to the quarries at Hindlow is still open for the transport of limestone, along with part of the Midland line through Peak Forest and down to the junctions at Chinley.

Mr G.B. Courtman began his railway career at Ashbourne as a junior clerk in 1914, retiring in 1961. He recalled the Ashbourne to Buxton line as being known to many as the 'Cope and Allen' line, due to the following state of affairs:

Station Master at Parsley Hay	Mr. Cope
Clerk at Hindlow, son-in-law of above	Mr. Fearn
Station Master at Hindlow, son of S.M. Parsley Hay	Mr Cope
Signalman at Hartington	Relation of one of the above.
Station Master at Tissington, brother of S.M. Parsley Hay	Mr. Cope
Station Master at Alsop-en-le-Dale	Mr. C. Allen
Porter at Thorpe Cloud. Brother of above	Mr. Allen

-Unbelievable, perhaps, but true!

Mr. G.F. Wilson worked as a goods guard over the line from 1944 to 1960 and was based at Uttoxeter. Uttoxeter train crews worked two passenger services from Monday to Saturdays out to Buxton and home again. Two freight trains were also worked over part of the line. One Down train changed over crews at Tissington or Alsop, with a Buxton crew working the Up train. The other train worked from Monday to Friday, the Down train changing with a Buxton crew at Parsley Hay.

Both the above gentlemen mention the following mishap which happened in the early thirties: An Up freight train was shunting in the sidings at Alsop. While the movements were being carried out, the signalman at Tissington rang to say that two or three wagons had just run through there and were heading at great speed towards Ashbourne. It was then realised that the wagons in question were part of those being shunted at Alsop-en-la-Dale, a load of tarred limestone, and it had not been noticed that they had 'got away'. From then on emergency regulations were carried out, and the signalman at Ashbourne No. 2 was advised that some wagons were heading towards him. The wagons could have been diverted from the main line at Ashbourne into a siding called the Milk Dock, but the signalman at Ashbourne No. 2 had a dilemma, because some workmen were repairing a wall ajacent to the siding and he knew that he did not have time to warn them to get clear and thought that the moving wagons would run them down with terrible consequences. He therefore decided to let them continue down the main line. Apparently the runaways passed through Ashbourne so quickly that the signalmen were not sure if there were two or three wagons. They were now heading for Clifton and Norbury. In Norbury station was the 12.50pm. Uttoxeter to Buxton passenger train. However, it was shunted clear and the wagons were derailed in a shunting loop. At a subsequent enquiry the signalman at Ashbourne No. 2 was disciplined for not diverting the wagons in to the Milk Dock siding.

Milk was of course one of the staple elements of traffic on the line, with regular daily runs from Derbyshire farms to Finsbury Park in North London until road transport took over. Although milk was plentiful, water was not on the porous soils, and lagoons, or meres had to be dug to provide water for the engines, ironic in view of the times in winter when snow would lie and block the line for weeks at a time; in 1947 it piled up to heights of twenty feet, and

Goods passing Norbury behind Class 4F No. 44271 on 5/9/63.
The Midland Railway Trust Ltd.

Clifton, for Mayfield station. Douglas Thompson

the unsuccessful idea was attempted of mounting an aircraft jet engine on a truck to try to blow the mounds away. Big guns were taken up the line to Alsop-en-le-Dale for testing on the moor during the last war, and various experiments have been carried out which involved the line and witnessed some unusual laboratory vehicles in transit.

Other books by the Author include:

'Railways in South Yorkshire.'
'The Great Northern & Great Eastern Joint Line.'
'The Dearne Valley Railway.'
'The Strathmore Railway.'
'Railways of East Yorkshire.' (Oakwood Press)

NOTES

NOTES

NOTES